Night Lights

By Tish Rabe
Based on a television script by Karen Moonah
Illustrated by Aristides Ruiz and Joe Mathieu

Random House 🏠 New York

TM and copyright © by Dr. Seuss Enterprises, L.P. 2014. All rights reserved. Published in the United States by Random House Children's Books, a division of Random House, Inc., 1745 Broadway, New York, NY 10019. Random House and the colophon are registered trademarks of Random House, Inc.

Based in part on *The Cat in the Hat Knows a Lot About That!* TV series (Episode 10) © CITH Productions, Inc. (a subsidiary of Portfolio Entertainment, Inc.), and Red Hat Animation, Ltd. (a subsidiary of Collingwood O'Hare Productions, Ltd.), 2012.

THE CAT IN THE HAT KNOWS A LOT ABOUT THAT! logo and word mark TM 2010 Dr. Seuss Enterprises, L.P., Portfolio Entertainment, Inc., and Collingwood O'Hare Productions, Ltd. All rights reserved. The PBS KIDS logo is a registered trademark of PBS. Both are used with permission. All rights reserved.

Broadcast in Canada by Treehouse™. Treehouse™ is a trademark of the Corus® Entertainment Inc. group of companies. All rights reserved.

Visit us on the Web! randomhouse.com/kids   Seussville.com   pbskids.org/catinthehat   treehousetv.com
Educators and librarians, for a variety of teaching tools, visit us at RHTeachersLibrarians.com
ISBN: 978-0-385-37116-2   Library of Congress Control Number: 2012954771
MANUFACTURED IN CHINA
10 9 8 7 6 5 4 3 2
First Edition

"Cool shadow shape,
Sally. Is it . . . *a carrot*?"
"Nick," Sally said,
"can't you see it's a parrot?
There's the head and the beak.
There's the tail and the wings."
"Sometimes shadow shapes," Nick said,
"look like different things."

"Shadow shapes!" cried the Cat.
"Oh, they're such fun to do!
Can you tell what shape
I am making for you?"

"An octopus?" said Nick.
"A spider? A chair?
A snake on a rake?
A big teddy bear?"

"It's a teapot," said Sally,
"with a very long spout!"
Then all of a sudden . . .

. . . their flashlight went out!

"Oh no!" Sally said.
"It's dark here at night."
"Fireflies," said the Cat,
"will give us some light.

"Press the Shrinkamadoodle!
And we'll be the right size
to go get some light
from some bright fireflies."

They alit in a bush
that sparkled with light.
"Fireflies," said the Cat,
"flash their lights in the night.

"There's my friend Shimmer
up high in the sky.
She's a glowing and beautiful,
bright firefly!"

"Hello, Cat," said Shimmer.
"I'm so glad to see you!
I've lost my friend Glimmer.
I don't know what to do!"

The Cat hollered, "Glimmer!"
Shimmer said, "Sorry, Cat,
but we fireflies don't call
each other like that.

"We flash our lights
in a pattern, you see.
Glimmer knows this light pattern
is coming from me.

"Look! Now I see
my friend Glimmer's own light.
But I think he's in trouble.
His light isn't right.

"His light isn't flashing
with its usual glow!
Glimmer needs us to help him.
Oh, hurry! Let's go!"

"Shimmer!" said Glimmer.
"I'm glad you came back.
I'm stuck and don't want
to be some spider's snack!"

"Don't worry," the Cat said.
"Tonight you're in luck.
My Web-snipper-ma-clipper
will get you unstuck."

"Thank you!" said Glimmer.
"Now what can we do?
You helped us, so tell me,
how can we help *you*?"

The Cat said, "Come with us
and bring your bright light
so we can have more
shadow-shape fun tonight.

"Fireflies shine with
a natural light.
They use it to call
to each other at night.

"And thanks to the brilliant
light that they throw,
we get to put on a fun . . .

". . . shadow show!"